What Crosses The Mind

well, my mind, maybe yours

Jazmine Greene

BookLeaf Publishing
India | USA | UK

Made with ❤ on the BookLeaf Publishing Platform
www.bookleafpub.in
www.bookleafpub.com

Dedication

My safe place.

Preface

Acknowledgements

1. My Shadow

I see you on a wall
I see you when I walk
When I lie down, I see you over there

Do you need anything?
Do you take bits and pieces of me?

You don't taste
You don't feel

Do you wish to exist
Instead of living on a wall
A sidewalk
Or inanimate objects

What is your purpose?

2. To be Remembered

I like to believe that when my time comes
I'll be remembered
For who I was

To the people who cared and loved me

To be remembered for the words I wrote
Whether it inspired others
Or
You were simply nice and read my poetry

We are many things in people's eyes
And I hope
In the eyes of others

I was someone decent to you
Kind
Respectful
Caring
A friend when needed
A good sister
A good daughter
A thoughtful person

Someone worthy

I like to believe that when my time comes
In my poetry, these words
It will matter to someone
Anyone

So, how would you like to be remembered?

3. A conversation in my head about my memory

Let me in

I'm ready for you
Whatever may come
I will protect us
You know, I couldn't then
But now I can

Let me in...please

We feel this pressure inside
It alright
We can feel
But we shouldn't tuck you away
This is scary for me
as well

Let me remember

4. Sad Girl

This sadness within me
The one constant that never leaves me

My sadness, and I know where we stand
I wish I didn't have my sadness all the time

I want to feel happy
Be content in my life

But it feels like a weight on my chest when I am happy
And it doesn’t feel right to be just content
It doesn't feel normal

So I lean into my sadness because that feels normal,
right

There is this internal struggle that I have
In my head

Hopefully one day

This sadness will be nothing but an acquaintance

5. Mirror...Mirror..Who's Looking Back?

Who are you?
Who am I?

Do you spend time
Knowing yourself
Mirrors, reflections
Self-awareness

I didn't start self-reflecting until my mid-30s

I've concluded that I never truly knew myself

Some layers make up me

But Jazmine as a whole
At times I feel like a damn stranger in my own body

I stare at a mirror now, and I see myself
But something feels off
It's distant

When I look back on my life
I never look at myself

Glimpses here and there

Do you ever look back on yourself
Did you ever stare at a mirror seeking answers

Who am I?
Who are you?

6. Wondering

People walking
To places
To whomever or wherever

They look at their surroundings
And some may see the same
Others will see something else

Do you often wonder what others see?

We all feel so many emotions

Do you often wonder what others feel?

There are these questions, and sometimes we may never
Have the answers to

And I guess we have to be ok with the unknown
But that doesn't mean we don't stop asking

7. Giving up...Maybe... Wanted to....But Didn't

The idea of giving up seemed so easy to me
To throw in the towel
And simply just be..I don't know, just didn't want this anymore
Whatever was left, that person would have been a shell of me

Not only would I have lost myself
But the idea of who I was
The creative side of me
My dreams
Then I would have allowed my mental state to eat me alive

During that, I was ready for that darkness
There were times when I wanted to feel empty
Be nothing

Made decisions that I knew were necessary

Therapy, how I needed you, but was too nervous to dive in
Faced my fear, it helped make things clear in my life

Talking to someone who knows what they are doing is a
wonderful relief

Medicated, the one thing I never thought I would have
done
I'm so happy I did
For the first time in a long time, my depression is not
toying with me
The anxiety that riddles me is at bay.
After a whole year on this, I came to terms with who I
was
And who I will never be again

Being a work in progress is who I am

Always trying is who I am
Never dampening my dreams
Always let the creativity shine

Be that beacon of hope, love, mindfulness, and
happiness.
Is what I need to do

The idea of giving up became a distant dream to me.

8. Crying

I'm crying
I'm writing as I'm crying
Just because
Why not
Im broken
Please let me remember more
Please
Please
I promise I will be okay

9. Its Time (memories are bitch so is childhood trauma)

I was a child
A little girl

I asked to do other things
Why did I ask
Did I enjoy what he did
Will I ever remember more

What if I did
What does that make me?

There is so much I can't remember
What did he do
How bad was it

The touching and me kicking I remember

My body feels so damn anxious when I try to go back

I don't think I truly trust myself

I'm pretty sure I don't like myself

Maybe because I never actually saw myself

10. Forgive Yourself

I never realized that when looking back
How much of my childhood
That I don't remember

It's all blank

Even when I try
My body becomes anxious

Saying I'm ready
It is different from my body being ready

How do I make this body ready?
For whatever may come

I will try to forgive you
For betraying me when I was younger

11. i’m sorry

What a lovely surprise, you are finally putting me first.
Am I not important?

I am sorry. You are such a massive piece of my soul.
And I put you on the back burner for so long
My first true passion is you, and I began to let it dwindle

My Writing

Yes me! We created poetry together, stories. I gave you life, and you were leaving me. When you needed me most, I was there. When you thought I left you for good, I never did. I don’t know when it began, but we became distant. Strangers in the night.

I have so much to say, but then you weren’t ready
Are you ready now?

I'm starting to unravel in a good way.
Breakdowns and more breakdowns
And so much damn crying

The more I open myself up

The more I know myself
Truly seeing myself for the first time

I never viewed myself as important
Underneath all of this, I hated myself
I began to let you go because it was easy
Because I didn't love you like I should have

We are one, I know that now
I can’t survive without you
Letting you down was because I was letting myself down
Putting you on the back burner was because that's where
I put myself

I am not important, so why shouldn't you be?
I have been so wrong

I am important, and so are you
The photography, the painting, and everything else in
between
Overshadowed you.

12. Just Listen

Do you ever just take a moment and listen to yourself
Not the voice in your head if you have one

But actually, listen to the sounds you make
And the way you speak
How you dialogue

Or just listen to the sounds
That you normally don't listen to
Maybe the way you chew
You take a drink
Do I slurp too long
Do I need to make a sound after every sip
And if I do, is it that good

When you're sitting by yourself
Do you talk to your TV
Do you talk out loud
If you do it in your voice
Or in an accent

When you're sitting alone
Make random sounds
Listen to how you breathe

How do you laugh when something is funny
Listen to your body crack and realize every crack in every bone is very distinctive in sound

Feeling the wind from my ears from my blanket when I cover myself, that's an interesting comforting sound

If you ever get bored, take a moment and just listen

13. Clarity/Confusion

I understand nothing
And yet everything

There is this space
Where clarity
An confusion
Co exists

In those times, sit in those moments
Let everything become confused and clear
Let your mind embrace what will come
Let that confusion feed into you

Once you allow the feast

Begin to let it all go

You will be exhausted, stressed, and downright ready to give up

When that time comes
You take you have learned
You search
You grow

You become what you need to be, the best version of yourself

Clarity and Confusion normally do not come hand and hand

But given the opportunity, if it does

Let it so

In your time of need, they will be your anchors
Hold you down

Because in that moment of space, you need to be ready and steady.

14. We Must

We are tied to our jobs
Obligations

Not disappointing others
While not doing the same to ourselves

Disappointing others should matter if only those people truly depend on you
If they don't, then worry about it

Disappointing yourself must be a top priority, as I mean
Taking care of yourself
Making sure you put yourself first

You matter

When we are not important to ourselves
That's where things fall between the cracks

Without noticing at first
You begin to lose who you are
You lose all sense of what makes you the person you should be for yourself

When you self-reflect and stare into a mirror
You may feel like a stranger
Feel this disconnect

We aren't tied to our job
If we feel as such, maybe it's time for a change

We must be our obligation

We must treat ourselves with every ounce of respect.

15. A lie for answers

Let us begin with a lie
I will tell you this, there will be some truth in it

Please understand
This is the only way

I must protect myself

Little do you know, the better we both will be in the end.

I promise you this,s in the lies you will find what you are looking for

16. Welcome

Welcome to whatever this is right now
I don't know
Will I ever
    I would hope so
Where do I start
    Where is the beginning
Or the middle
For sure, I know what I want the ending to be

Anyway..

Welcome to those who have never read what I've written before
    Welcome, and I hope you stay for a while
While you're here, check out my other two books
Pieces of a complex mind and Words on paper

Welcome to my mind, my soul, and my heart.
I like to think of it as a beautiful mess where ideas and stories begin, and the middle is my writing.

Welcome to my poetry. I have so much more to show you all

17. Peace, Heart, Mind, You

Peace is what many seek in this world. I know do

My heart is searching for a connection.

The mind needs clarity because, at times, it goes cloudy

I want you, oh, I'm pretty sure this feeling is being in love

The heart settles in a certain way as it finds its home
The mind, this mind, is willing to take whatever may come

You, my heart, and my mind coexist to build a peace I've never known before.

Peace, Heart, Mind. You

Those words have their meaning
What I desire
crosses my mind many times
It's the idea of having those feelings

Creating tranquility

A heart at home
The mind is finally opening
Finding that right person

I'd always wonder if having those feelings or thoughts
has such.
Iis what it means to be truly in love.

18. Hey soul, I have some questions

Is death the end
If so
What happens to the soul
Does it die as well

Will the soul transfer to another
Or just fade away

What makes up a soul
Does the soul feel

A soulmate
How do two people just know that they are each other's

People say it aches, in pain, in pursuit

A soul, your soul, my soul, our soul

what's a soul

19. Liberation (its time)

Say it
Write it
Fucking feel it

Just let everyhting the fuck out

Speak it
Express it
Fucking feel it

Take a nap
Eat some good food
Workout a bit

Do what is necessary to make sure you
Fucking feel it
Then let that shit go

20. Love

Can you remember the last time you were loved
Unconditionally

Or been in love

Where, without a question or a doubt

What did that feel
Was it everything you could imagine

And if you haven’t
What stopped you
What's stopping you

Is there a voice in your head keeping you from trying

Are you scared to put yourself out there?

Or maybe rejection

Love is love

But in love
It can tear you apart

Break you down
It makes you hate everything
Feel anything

Will you allow yourself to love
To be loved
Allow that love in return

21. Happiness

Hello Happiness
Welcome to the work in progress
It's nice to see you again
Feels rather wonderful

My perspective on life is clearer
The hope that lives within me
Is ever-flowing

Thank you for not giving up on me

Whether you feel me or right
I'm always with you
Giving you what you need
When you are ready for it.
I cannot act as a false hope to
So the times I'm not shining bright
I am not abandoning you
Giving you some space
Just until truly ready

Always keep working on yourself

Standing still isn't for you
Change can equal a lifetime of happiness
One day, you will not be a sad girl

www.ingramcontent.com/pod-product-compliance
Lightning Source LLC
Chambersburg PA
CBHW051748130826
49812CB00033B/1049
* 9 7 8 9 3 7 0 9 2 3 6 4 5 *